by Iain Gray

Lang**Syne**
PUBLISHING
WRITING *to* REMEMBER

Lang**Syne**
PUBLISHING
WRITING *to* REMEMBER

E-mail: info@lang-syne.co.uk

Distributed in the Republic of Ireland by Portfolio Group,
Kilbarrack Ind. Est. Kilbarrack, Dublin 5.
T:00353(01) 839 4918 F:00353(01) 839 5826
sales@portfoliogroup.ie
www.portfoliogroup.ie

Design by Dorothy Meikle
Printed by Martins the Printers, Berwick-upon-Tweed

© Lang Syne Publishers Ltd 2012

All rights reserved. No part of this publication may be reproduced, stored
or introduced into a retrieval system, or transmitted in any form or by any
means (electronic, mechanical, photocopying, recording or otherwise) without
the prior written permission of Lang Syne Publishers Ltd.

ISBN 978-1-85217-296-1

Burke

MOTTO:
One king, one faith, one law.

CREST:
A mountain cat, collared and chained.

NAME variations include:
de Burgh
de Burca
Bourke
Burgh
Burk

Chapter one:
Origins of Irish surnames

**According to an old saying, there are two types of Irish –
those who actually are Irish and those who wish they were.**

This sentiment is only one example of the allure that the
high romance and drama of the proud nation's history holds
for thousands of people scattered across the world today.

It's a sad fact, however, that the vast majority of Irish
surnames are found far beyond Irish shores, rather than on
the Emerald Isle itself.

The population stood at around eight million souls in
1841, but today it stands at fewer than six million.

This is mainly a tragic consequence of the potato
famine, also known as the Great Hunger, which devastated
Ireland between 1845 and 1849.

The Irish peasantry had become almost wholly reliant
for basic sustenance on the potato, first introduced from the
Americas in the seventeenth century.

When the crop was hit by a blight, at least 800,000
people starved to death while an estimated two million
others were forced to seek a new life far from their native
shores – particularly in America, Canada, and Australia.

The effects of the potato blight continued until about
1851, by which time a firm pattern of emigration had
become established.

Ireland's loss, however, was to the gain of the countries in which the immigrants settled, contributing enormously, as their descendants do today, to the well being of the nations in which their forefathers settled.

But those who were forced through dire circumstance to establish a new life in foreign parts never forgot their roots, or the proud heritage and traditions of the land that gave them birth.

Nor do their descendants.

It is a heritage that is inextricably bound up in the colourful variety of Irish names themselves – and the origin and history of these names forms an integral part of the vibrant drama that is the nation's history, one of both glorious fortune and tragic misfortune.

This history is well documented, and one of the most important and fascinating of the earliest sources are *The Annals of the Four Masters*, compiled between 1632 and 1636 by four friars at the Franciscan Monastery in County Donegal.

Compiled from earlier sources, and purporting to go back to the Biblical Deluge, much of the material takes in the mythological origins and history of Ireland and the Irish.

This includes tales of successive waves of invaders and settlers such as the Fomorians, the Partholonians, the Nemedians, the Fir Bolgs, the Tuatha De Danann, and the Laigain.

Of particular interest are the *Milesian Genealogies*,

because the majority of Irish clans today claim a descent from either Heremon, Ir, or Heber – three of the sons of Milesius, a king of what is now modern day Spain.

These sons invaded Ireland in the second millennium B.C, apparently in fulfilment of a mysterious prophecy received by their father.

This Milesian lineage is said to have ruled Ireland for nearly 3,000 years, until the island came under the sway of England's King Henry II in 1171 following what is known as the Cambro-Norman invasion.

This is an important date not only in Irish history in general, but for the effect the invasion subsequently had for Irish surnames.

'Cambro' comes from the Welsh, and 'Cambro-Norman' describes those Welsh knights of Norman origin who invaded Ireland.

But they were invaders who stayed, inter-marrying with the native Irish population and founding their own proud dynasties that bore Cambro-Norman names such as Archer, Barbour, Brannagh, Fitzgerald, Fitzgibbon, Fleming, Joyce, Plunkett, and Walsh – to name only a few.

These 'Cambro-Norman' surnames that still flourish throughout the world today form one of the three main categories in which Irish names can be placed – those of Gaelic-Irish, Cambro-Norman, and Anglo-Irish.

Previous to the Cambro-Norman invasion of the twelfth century, and throughout the earlier invasions and settlement of those wild bands of sea rovers known as the Vikings in the eighth and ninth centuries, the population of the island was relatively small, and it was normal for a person to be identified through the use of only a forename.

But as population gradually increased and there were many more people with the same forename, surnames were adopted to distinguish one person, or one community, from another.

Individuals identified themselves with their own particular tribe, or 'tuath', and this tribe – that also became known as a clann, or clan – took its name from some distinguished ancestor who had founded the clan.

The Gaelic-Irish form of the name Kelly, for example, is Ó Ceallaigh, or O'Kelly, indicating descent from an original 'Ceallaigh', with the 'O' denoting 'grandson of.' The name was later anglicised to Kelly.

The prefix 'Mac' or 'Mc', meanwhile, as with the clans of the Scottish Highlands, denotes 'son of.'

Although the Irish clans had much in common with their Scottish counterparts, one important difference lies in what are known as 'septs', or branches, of the clan.

Septs of Scottish clans were groups who often bore an entirely different name from the clan name but were under the clan's protection.

In Ireland, septs were groups that shared the same name and who could be found scattered throughout the four provinces of Ulster, Leinster, Munster, and Connacht.

The 'golden age' of the Gaelic-Irish clans, infused as their veins were with the blood of Celts, pre-dates the Viking invasions of the eighth and ninth centuries and the Norman invasion of the twelfth century, and the sacred heart of the country was the Hill of Tara, near the River Boyne, in County Meath.

Known in Gaelic as 'Teamhar na Rí', or Hill of Kings, it was the royal seat of the 'Ard Rí Éireann', or High King of Ireland, to whom the petty kings, or chieftains, from the island's provinces were ultimately subordinate.

It was on the Hill of Tara, beside a stone pillar known as the Irish 'Lia Fáil', or Stone of Destiny, that the High Kings were inaugurated and, according to legend, this stone would emit a piercing screech that could be heard all over Ireland when touched by the hand of the rightful king.

The Hill of Tara is today one of the island's main tourist attractions.

Opposition to English rule over Ireland, established in the wake of the Cambro-Norman invasion, broke out frequently and the harsh solution adopted by the powerful forces of the Crown was to forcibly evict the native Irish from their lands.

These lands were then granted to Protestant colonists, or 'planters', from Britain.

Many of these colonists, ironically, came from Scotland and were the descendants of the original 'Scotti', or 'Scots', who gave their name to Scotland after migrating there in the fifth century A.D., from the north of Ireland.

Colonisation entailed harsh penal laws being imposed on the majority of the native Irish population, stripping them practically of all of their rights.

The Crown's main bastion in Ireland was Dublin and its environs, known as the Pale, and it was the dispossessed peasantry who lived outside this Pale, desperately striving to eke out a meagre living.

It was this that gave rise to the modern-day expression of someone or something being 'beyond the pale'.

Attempts were made to stamp out all aspects of the ancient Gaelic-Irish culture, to the extent that even to bear a Gaelic-Irish name was to invite discrimination.

This is why many Gaelic-Irish names were anglicised with, for example, and noted above, Ó Ceallaigh, or O'Kelly, being anglicised to Kelly.

Succeeding centuries have seen strong revivals of Gaelic-Irish consciousness, however, and this has led to many families reverting back to the original form of their name, while the language itself is frequently found on the fluent tongues of an estimated 90,000 to 145,000 of the island's population.

Ireland's turbulent history of religious and political strife is one that lasted well into the twentieth century, a landmark century that saw the partition of the island into the twenty-six counties of the independent Republic of

Ireland, or Eire, and the six counties of Northern Ireland, or Ulster.

Dublin, originally founded by Vikings, is now a vibrant and truly cosmopolitan city while the proud city of Belfast is one of the jewels in the crown of Ulster.

It was Saint Patrick who first brought the light of Christianity to Ireland in the fifth century A.D.

Interpretations of this Christian message have varied over the centuries, often leading to bitter sectarian conflict – but the many intricately sculpted Celtic Crosses found all over the island are symbolic of a unity that crosses the sectarian divide.

It is an image that fuses the 'old gods' of the Celts with Christianity.

All the signs from the early years of this new millennium indicate that sectarian strife may soon become a thing of the past – with the Irish and their many kinsfolk across the world, be they Protestant or Catholic, finding common purpose in the rich tapestry of their shared heritage.

Chapter two:
Of high ambition

Although of original Norman stock, descendants of the Burkes who first settled in Ireland in the late twelfth century assimilated the native culture to such an extent that some were referred to as having become 'more Irish than the Irish.'

This was a description bestowed on them as they came to identify with the land in which they had settled, acquiring rich territories and honours along the way.

But it was in the form of ambitious and ruthless invaders and adventurers that the Burkes, or de Burghs or de Burgos, first descended on the Emerald Isle.

This was in the wake of the Cambro-Norman invasion of the island in 1169 and the subsequent consolidation of the power of the English Crown under which the island acquired the status of a colony.

Henry II had landed in Ireland at the head of a large army in October of 1171 with the aim of curbing the power of his Cambro-Norman barons.

But war between king and barons was averted when they submitted to the royal will, promising homage and allegiance in return for holding the territories they had conquered in the king's name, while Henry also received the reluctant submission and homage of many of the Irish chieftains.

This led to the creation of three 'separate' Irelands.

These were the territories of the privileged and powerful Norman barons and their retainers, the Ireland of the disaffected Gaelic-Irish who held lands unoccupied by the Normans, and the Pale – comprised of Dublin itself and a substantial area of its environs ruled over by an English elite.

Among those Norman nobles who were to benefit greatly from the rich pickings that Ireland had to offer, at the expense of the native clans, was William de Burgh, a brother of the powerful Hubert de Burgh, who held the post of Justiciar of England.

The brothers, whose forefathers had come to England in the wake of the Norman Conquest of 1066, proudly claimed a descent from no less an illustrious figure than Charlemagne ('Charles the Great'), the king of the Franks who came to rule over a vast empire that included Gaul, Italy, and parts of Germany and Spain, and who was crowned Emperor by the Pope in 800 A.D.

The highly ambitious William de Burgh arrived in Ireland from England in about 1185, and one indication of how he rapidly acquired rich territories is that the Irish annals refer to him as 'William the Conqueror.'

Thanks in part to the influence of his brother, William de Burgh was made governor of Limerick.

While many of the territories he subsequently acquired were carved out by the brutal use of fire and sword he also, in common with other Norman settlers, made an important dynastic alliance with the native Irish through marriage.

This was through marrying a daughter of the O'Brien king of Thomond, in the northern reaches of the province of Munster.

It was through such marriages that the Burkes and other original Norman families absorbed the culture and lifestyle of the Gaelic-Irish.

Some of the Burkes, indeed, adopted the Irish law known as Brehon and spawned their own septs, or branches, that included those of MacWilliam Iochtar, in Co. Mayo, MacWilliam Uachtar, in Galway, in addition to those of MacSeoinin and MacDavid.

William de Burgh, meanwhile, progenitor of those Burkes who were destined to thrive in Ireland, also turned his attention to the province of Connacht, carving out territories there after engaging in protracted and bloody warfare with the O'Connor kings of the province.

He died in 1204, perhaps from leprosy, but not before having laid the basis of de Burgh, or Burke, power in Ireland.

He was followed by his equally ambitious and ruthless son Richard de Burgh, born in about 1193, and who became not only Lord of Connacht and Trim, in Co. Meath, but also Viceroy of Ireland.

Continuing the policy of important dynastic marriage, he married the daughter of an O'Connor chieftain of Connacht.

Richard died in 1243 and, obviously a chip off the old Burke block, his son Walter de Burgh acquired the powerful Earldom of Ulster in 1263 through marriage – not, however, into a native Irish clan, but through his marriage to a daughter of the influential Anglo-Norman family of de Lacy.

One of his legacies can still be seen on the landscape today – in the form of the imposing ruins of what was once the magnificent Dunluce Castle, between Portballintrae and Portrush in Ulster's Co. Antrim.

Built by Walter de Burgh, and visited by hundreds of tourists every year, it is now in the care of Northern Ireland's Environment and Heritage Service.

The Earldom of Ulster was lost to the family in the mid fourteenth century when the only heir, Elizabeth de Burgo, married the Duke of Clarence.

The duke, who was of the Royal House of York, became the Earl of Ulster, a title that has passed to Britain's royal family of today.

Burkes also established a powerful presence in Co. Galway – indeed some sources assert that it was Richard de Burgh who founded the city of Galway – with Ulick de Burgo created Earl of Clanricarde by Henry VIII in 1543.

The fine castle of the Clanricardes at Portumna passed in 1916 to Viscount Lascelles, the husband of George V's daughter, the Princess Mary, following the death of the last Marquess of Clanricarde.

Meanwhile other titles that had been acquired by the family included Viscounts Mayo, Lords Mayo, and Barons Naas.

Turning back the pages of history the Burkes certainly did not have their sorrows to seek in controlling those territories they had acquired.

The annals tell of how a Burke was despatched to collect rent in their Connacht territory from the O'Flahertys.

Treated to a feast in the O'Flaherty bastion of Aughanure Castle in Oughterard, the Burke emissary raised the question of the rent – only to be plunged into the river that ran beneath the castle after his hosts, in true Indiana Jones fashion, released a concealed catch in the flagstone on which his chair rested.

His head was then cut off and, described as 'O'Flaherty's rent', sent back to the Burkes.

One indispensable tool of genealogical researchers is *A Genealogical and Heraldic Dictionary of the Peerage and Baronetage of the United Kingdom* – more familiarly known as *Burke's Peerage*.

It was the original creation of John Burke, born in 1787, and his son Sir John Bernard Burke, born in 1814.

With justifiable pride in their roots, the Burkes' original entry for their own family tells of how they held 'by conquest and royal grant, whole territories in the counties Galway, Mayo, Roscommon, Tipperary, and Limerick; and so extended were its possessions, that its very cadets became persons of wealth, and were founders of distinguished houses themselves.'

One of the most noted of these 'persons of wealth' was Richard Burke, known as Richard an Iarainn, or 'Iron Richard', because of the vast wealth he accrued from his iron mines and iron works on his lands at Burrishoole, in Co. Mayo.

He was the second husband of the famed Gráinne Ni Mháille, or Grace O'Malley, the daughter of an O'Malley chief and who became known as 'the Pirate Queen', or the 'Sea Queen of Connacht.'

The O'Malleys, tenants of the Burkes in the barony of Murrisk, in the southwest of Co. Mayo, were daring seafarers, and young Grace would often accompany her father on his piratical activities.

These included stopping and boarding trading vessels en route to the thriving trading port of Galway City and demanding payment before allowing them to proceed further.

She married 'Iron Richard' in 1567, following the death of her first husband, and their son Tibbot Burke, known as 'Tioboid na Long', or 'Tibbot of the Ship', was actually born at sea.

The English took Tibbot hostage in his youth and, when he returned to his native land, he was destined to become embroiled in one of the island's most bloody and decisive battles against English rule.

Chapter three:

Revolt and assassination

Rebellion had broken out in Ireland in 1541 when England's HenryVIII not only peremptorily declared himself King of Ireland, but also announced that as such, all Irish lands were now Crown property.

Adding fuel to the flames of the revolt was his religious Reformation that denied the supremacy of the Roman Catholic Church and the policy of 'planting' Protestants on Irish land.

Matters for the Irish only went from bad to worse during the subsequent reign of Henry's daughter, Queen Elizabeth I, with a growing emphasis on the policy of plantation first instigated by her father.

This was a practice that would accelerate during the reign of her successor James I (James VI of Scotland), and in the grim aftermath of the Cromwellian conquest of the island in 1649.

The native Irish population by no means submitted to its fate lightly, and the island was frequently wracked by violent explosions of insurrection and rebellion against the forces of the Crown.

Among those who fequently found themselves in revolt were branches of the Burkes who resented the increasing encroachment on their powers by the Crown, and who identified more with the soil of Ireland than they did with Westminster or the Anglo-Irish establishment in Dublin.

Even as early as 1534, according to one source, 'the ruling de Burgh families have so far deviated from English civil standards as to be indistinguishable from Gaelic chieftains.'

One of the bloodiest of the rebellions was the Nine Years War, from 1594 to 1603, and the rebel leaders, known as the Confederate Chiefs, received aid from King Philip III of Spain in the form of a Spanish invasion force that landed at Kinsale in 1601 under the command of Don Juan del Águila.

Joined by a rebel army from Ulster, in the north, it was defeated following the siege of Kinsale, however, and Águila surrendered to Lord Mountjoy, Queen Elizabeth's Lord Deputy for Ireland.

While some Burkes had rallied to the doomed cause of the rebels Tibbald Burke, perhaps frustrated that he had failed to assume the lordship of Mayo on his return to Ireland, supported the English cause and fought at Kinsale.

His loyalty paid dividends when he was later created 1st Viscount Mayo – but the title only survived until the mid-eighteenth century.

The final death knell of the ancient Gaelic order came in the late seventeenth century in the form of what is known in Ireland as Cogadh an Dá Rí, or The War of the Two Kings.

Also known as the Williamite War in Ireland or the Jacobite War in Ireland, it was sparked off in 1688 when the Stuart monarch James II (James VII of Scotland) was deposed and fled into exile in France.

The Protestant William of Orange and his wife Mary were invited to take up the thrones of Scotland, Ireland, and England – but James still had significant support in Ireland where a series of military encounters followed, culminating in his defeat by an army commanded by William at the battle of the Boyne on July 12, 1689.

The Williamite forces besieged Limerick and James's supporters were forced into surrender in September of 1691.

A peace treaty known as the Treaty of Limerick followed, under which those willing to swear an oath of loyalty to William were allowed to remain in their native land.

Those reluctant to do so, including many Burkes, were allowed to seek exile on foreign shores.

A further flight overseas occurred following an abortive rebellion in 1798, while Burkes were among the many thousands of Irish who were forced to seek a new life many thousands of miles from their native land during the famine known as The Great Hunger, caused by a failure of the potato crop between 1845 and 1849.

One of the most prominent Burkes whose family remained in Ireland was Thomas Henry Burke, the Permanent Undersecretary at the Irish Office who was stabbed to death along with Lord Frederick Cavendish, the newly appointed Chief Secretary for Ireland, as the pair strolled through Dublin's Phoenix Park on May 6, 1882.

Members of a republican organisation known as the Irish National Invincibles were responsible for the attack.

One particularly infamous Burke was William Burke, born in 1792 in Urney, Co. Tyrone, who, along with fellow Irishman William Hare, committed at least seventeen gruesome murders in Edinburgh.

Burke had come to Scotland in about 1827 and after a series of labouring jobs found lodgings in the Scottish capital in the home of fellow labourer Hare.

This was a time when fresh corpses were in great demand from medical colleges for dissection – but the only ones legally available were those of executed felons.

This led to the practice of 'body snatching' from graveyards, but Burke and Hare supplied the lucrative demand by smothering or suffocating innocent souls they had lured to the lodging house, leaving no visible injury – a method of killing that came to be known as 'Burking'.

The forces of the law eventually caught up with them and, along with accomplices that included Burke's mistress and Hare's wife, they were brought to trial.

Hare was granted immunity from prosecution for agreeing to testify against Burke, while the charges against the women were found not proven – but Burke was found guilty, sentenced to death, and hanged on January 28, 1829.

His corpse, ironically, was given to the Edinburgh Medical College for Dissection, while his skeleton is on display to this day within the medical school of the Royal College of Surgeons of Edinburgh.

Chapter four:

On the world stage

On a rather less infamous note than the murderer William Burke, bearers of the name, in all its rich variety of spellings, have achieved fame and distinction in a number of fields, not least that of music.

Born in 1948 in Pergamino, Argentina, Christopher James Davison is better known by his stage name of **Chris de Burgh**.

The talented singer and songwriter is the son of the former British diplomat Charles Davison and Maeve Emily de Burgh, whose father was General Sir Eric de Burgh.

The Davison family left Argentina to later settle in the 12th century Bargy Castle, in Ireland, that had been bought by Sir Eric.

This branch of the Irish de Burghs trace their roots back to the Norman nobleman Hubert de Burgh and, proud of his heritage, the singer and songwriter later adopted 'de Burgh' as his stage name.

His many hits include the 1986 *The Lady in Red*, while his daughter Rosanna Davison won the Miss World Competition in 2003.

Inducted into the Songwriters Hall of Fame in 1970, **Joseph Burke** was the American actor, composer and pianist who was born in 1884 in Philadelphia.

A prolific songwriter and composer of film scores, he composed the 1929 *Gold Diggers of Broadway*, while his memorable songs include the Gene Austin hit *Carolina Moon*, the 1930 Nat Shilkret song *Dancing with Tears in My Eyes*, the 1947 *Rambling Rose*, and *Tip Toe Through the Tulips*. He died in 1950.

In contemporary times **Clem Burke**, born Clement Bozewski in 1955 in Bayonne, New Jersey, was the drummer for the American pop band Blondie, that featured singer Debbie Harry, while he has also played for artistes that include Bob Dylan, The Eurythmics, and Iggy Pop.

He was inducted into the Rock and Roll Hall of Fame in 2006.

A bandleader for the recordings of singers such as Mel Tormé and Ella Fitzgerald, **Sonny Burke** was the musician born in Scranton, Pennsylvania, in 1914 and who died in 1980.

He worked as a band arranger during the 1940s and 1950s for top musicians such as the Jimmy Dorsey and Charlie Spinks bands, while for a time he was musical director of Reprise Records and responsible for many of Frank Sinatra's recordings.

Also in the United States **Raymond Burke**, born in 1904 in New Orleans and who died in 1986, was a leading jazz clarinettist.

Back in the Burke homeland of Ireland **Joe Burke**, born in 1939, is the accordion player from Co. Galway who is a two-times winner of the All-Ireland Senior Accordion Championship.

On the stage **David Burke**, born in Liverpool in 1934, is the English actor best known for his role as Dr Watson in the 1980s British television series *The Adventurers of Sherlock Holmes*.

Best known as the host of the Australian lifestyle programme *Burke's Backyard*, that ran from 1987 to 2004, **Don Burke** is the Australian television personality who was born in 1947, while **Kathy Burke**, born in London in 1964 to Irish immigrant parents, is the actress and theatre director who has played both comedic and dramatic roles.

She won a Best Actress Award at the Cannes Film festival in 1997 for her role in the drama *Nil by Mouth*, while her television roles include that of Perry in the Harry Enfield comedy series, and in *Gimme Gimme Gimme*, that ran from 1999 to 2001.

Born in 1971 in Hartford, Connecticut, **Brooke Burke** is the American model and television personality best known as the host of the *Wild On!* travel series that ran from 1992 to 2002 and the 2005-2006 *Rock Star* series.

Delta Burke, born in 1956 in Orlando, Florida, is the American film and television actress best known for her role as Suzanne Sugerbaker in the U.S. sitcom *Designing Women*, for which she was the recipient of two consecutive Emmy nominations for Best Actress, in 1990 and 1991.

In the world of literature **James Lee Burke**, born in

Houston, Texas, in 1936, is the American writer best known for his Dave Robicheaux series of mysteries.

The recipient of an Edgar Award for Best Novel in 1990 for his novel *Black Cherry Blues* and for *Cimarron Rose* in 1998, his *Heaven's Prisoner* was filmed in 1996 starring Alec Baldwin, while his *In the Electric Mist with Confederate Dead* was filmed in 2007 starring Tommy Lee Jones.

An author, statesman, political theorist, orator and philosopher, **Edmund Burke** was born in Dublin in 1729.

Serving in the British House of Commons as a Whig Member of Parliament, he was an outspoken supporter of the American colonies in their dispute with Britain, while he was also a vociferous opponent of the French Revolution.

He is best known for his rather cumbersomely entitled *A Vindication of Natural Society: A View of the Miseries and Evils Arising to Mankind*, published in 1756, and for controversial *Reflections on the Revolution* in France, published seven years before his death in 1797.

In contemporary times **Peter Burke**, born in 1937, is the leading British historian whose many works include *The Italian Renaissance* and the 2002 *A Social History of Knowledge*.

Born in 1936 in Derry, Northern Ireland, **James Burke** is the author, television producer, and science historian who is a recipient of the prestigious Royal Television Society's gold and silver medals.

He is best known for the former BBC science series *Tomorrow's World* and the documentary series *Connections*.

In the field of exploration **Robert O'Hara Burke**, born in Co. Galway in 1821, was both a soldier and a police officer before he became an explorer.

Serving with the British Army and later with the Austrian Army, he returned to his native Ireland for a time and joined the Royal Irish Constabulary.

Ever footloose, he immigrated to Australia in 1853 and joined the Victoria police force.

He was appointed only seven years later to lead an expedition along with William Wills to cross the Australian continent from south to north.

The ill-fated expedition claimed the lives of several of its members, including Burke and Wills, although Burke is reckoned to have achieved his goal before he died of starvation and exposure.

The bodies of both men were later recovered and afforded a State Funeral in Melbourne.

On the field of battle **Admiral Arleigh Burke**, born in 1923 in Boulder, Colorado and who died in 1996, was the distinguished admiral of the U.S. Navy during the Second World War and the Korean War who later served as Chief of Naval Operations from 1955 until his retiral in 1961.

Born in 1747 in Hillsborough, North Carolina, **Thomas Burke** was the American doctor, lawyer, and statesman who was an active supporter of the American Revolution and who was imprisoned for a time by the British on James Island, near Charleston, South Carolina.

Burke County, in North Carolina, is named in his honour.

Born in Pennsylvania in 1830, **John Burke** was a Confederate adjutant general during the American Civil War of 1861 to 1865 and who also acted as a spy – on one occasion hiding under a lady's petticoats to avoid detection from Union soldiers who were chasing him.

In the creative world of art **Thomas Burke**, born in 1749 in Dublin, was a gifted Irish engraver and painter, while fellow Irishman **John Burke**, born in Clonmel, Co. Tipperary in 1946 and who died in 2006, was a noted sculptor.

Born in Connemara in 1838 **Augustus Burke** was the renowned artist who was a brother of Theodore Burke, 13th Baronet Burke of Glinsk, and Thomas Henry Burke, the Permanent Under Secretary at the Irish Office who was one of the two victims in the 1882 Phoenix Park murders.

The National Gallery of Ireland is home to two of his most famous paintings – *Connemara Girl* and *Connemara Landscape*.

Burkes have also excelled, and continue to excel, in the highly competitive world of sport.

Born in 1980 in Louisville, Kentucky, **Chris Burke** is a Major League Baseball player with, at the time of writing, the American Diamondbacks, while **John C. Burke**, born in 1970 in Durango, Colorado, was the Major League pitcher who played for the Colorado Rookies in 1996 and 1997.

In European football **Chris Burke**, born in Glasgow in 1983, is the Scottish professional footballer who won his first cap for his nation in 2006 and who, at the time of writing, plays for Rangers in the Scottish Premier League.

In rowing **Joseph Burk**, who died in 2008 at the age of 94, was the American oarsman and coach who was the U.S. and Canadian champion from 1937 to 1940.

On the rugby pitch **Matt Burke**, born in Sydney in 1973, is the Australian rugby union player who, at the time of writing, is the all-time second-highest scorer for Australia in international rugby.

In ice hockey **Sean Burke**, born in 1967 in Windsor, Ontario is the former Canadian professional goal tender who played for the men's national team at the 1988 Calgary Olympics.

On the athletic track **Thomas Burke**, born in 1875 and who died in 1929, was the first modern Olympic champion in the 100 and 400-metre races – taking gold in both events at the inaugural modern Olympic Games at Athens in 1896.

Burkes have also left their mark on the Wild West.

Born in 1852 in Princeton, Missouri, Martha Jane Cannary-Burke is better known as the American frontierswoman **Calamity Jane**.

A friend of Wild West legends such as Wild Bill Hickok,

she took the name Burke after marrying the Texan Clinton Burke.

By 1893 she was appearing as a rider and trick shooter in the famed Buffalo Bill's Wild West Show.

Calamity, who died in 1903, is buried in Mount Moriah Cemetery in South Dakota – next to her old friend and gunslinger Wild Bill Hickok.

Key dates in Ireland's history from the first settlers to the formation of the Irish Republic:

circa 7000 B.C.	Arrival and settlement of Stone Age people.
circa 3000 B.C.	Arrival of settlers of New Stone Age period.
circa 600 B.C.	First arrival of the Celts.
200 A.D.	Establishment of Hill of Tara, Co. Meath, as seat of the High Kings.
circa 432 A.D.	Christian mission of St. Patrick.
800-920 A.D.	Invasion and subsequent settlement of Vikings.
1002 A.D.	Brian Boru recognised as High King.
1014	Brian Boru killed at battle of Clontarf.
1169-1170	Cambro-Norman invasion of the island.
1171	Henry II claims Ireland for the English Crown.
1366	Statutes of Kilkenny ban marriage between native Irish and English.
1529-1536	England's Henry VIII embarks on religious Reformation.
1536	Earl of Kildare rebels against the Crown.
1541	Henry VIII declared King of Ireland.
1558	Accession to English throne of Elizabeth I.
1565	Battle of Affane.
1569-1573	First Desmond Rebellion.
1579-1583	Second Desmond Rebellion.
1594-1603	Nine Years War.
1606	Plantation' of Scottish and English settlers.
1607	Flight of the Earls.
1632-1636	Annals of the Four Masters compiled.
1641	Rebellion over policy of plantation and other grievances.
1649	Beginning of Cromwellian conquest.
1688	Flight into exile in France of Catholic Stuart monarch James II as Protestant Prince William of Orange invited to take throne of England along with his wife, Mary.
1689	William and Mary enthroned as joint monarchs; siege of Derry.
1690	Jacobite forces of James defeated by William at battle of the Boyne (July) and Dublin taken.

1691	Athlone taken by William; Jacobite defeats follow at Aughrim, Galway, and Limerick; conflict ends with Treaty of Limerick (October) and Irish officers allowed to leave for France.
1695	Penal laws introduced to restrict rights of Catholics; banishment of Catholic clergy.
1704	Laws introduced constricting rights of Catholics in landholding and public office.
1728	Franchise removed from Catholics.
1791	Foundation of United Irishmen republican movement.
1796	French invasion force lands in Bantry Bay.
1798	Defeat of Rising in Wexford and death of United Irishmen leaders Wolfe Tone and Lord Edward Fitzgerald.
1800	Act of Union between England and Ireland.
1803	Dublin Rising under Robert Emmet.
1829	Catholics allowed to sit in Parliament.
1845-1849	The Great Hunger: thousands starve to death as potato crop fails and thousands more emigrate.
1856	Phoenix Society founded.
1858	Irish Republican Brotherhood established.
1873	Foundation of Home Rule League.
1893	Foundation of Gaelic League.
1904	Foundation of Irish Reform Association.
1913	Dublin strikes and lockout.
1916	Easter Rising in Dublin and proclamation of an Irish Republic.
1917	Irish Parliament formed after Sinn Fein election victory.
1919-1921	War between Irish Republican Army and British Army.
1922	Irish Free State founded, while six northern counties remain part of United Kingdom as Northern Ireland, or Ulster; civil war; civil war up until 1923 between rival republican groups.
1949	Foundation of Irish Republic after all remaining constitutional links with Britain are severed.